Letters

Written by Jennifer Dryden
Illustrations by Steve Mack

FlashKids

New York

New York

An Imprint of Sterling Publishing
387 Park Avenue South
New York, NY 10016

ISBN 978-1-4114-5808-6 (paperback)

Distributed in Canada by Sterling Publishing
c/o Canadian Manda Group, 165 Dufferin Street
Toronto, Ontario, Canada M6K 3H6
Distributed in the United Kingdom by GMC Distribution Services
Castle Place, 166 High Street, Lewes, East Sussex, England BN7 1XU
Distributed in Australia by Capricorn Link (Australia) Pty. Ltd.
P.O. Box 704, Windsor, NSW 2756, Australia

For information about custom editions, special sales, and premium and corporate purchases, please contact
Sterling Special Sales at 800-805-5489 or specialsales@sterlingpublishing.com.

Manufactured in Canada
Lot #:
2 4 6 8 10 9 7 5 3 1
11/11

www.flashkids.com

Dear Parent,
Letters offers simple and complex activities that progress from drawing letter strokes and writing uppercase and lowercase letters to spelling simple words. As you work through this book with your child, offer guidance on difficult activities, but allow your preschooler to work through challenges independently. When the workbook is complete, reward your child with the certificate provided on page 79. For free downloads and fun activity ideas, visit www.flashkids.com.

Have your child make an "L" shape with his or her pointer finger and thumb. Lay the pencil at the crease of the "L" shape, allowing the tip of the pencil to rest on the middle finger. Ask your child to pinch his or her pointer finger and thumb to the pencil so it is comfortable. Begin writing! Reinforce the proper way to hold a pencil if your child is having trouble.

Corn stalks grow tall and straight.
Draw vertical lines from dot (●) to dot (●).

Fences keep the animals from wandering.
Draw horizontal lines from dot (●) to dot (●).

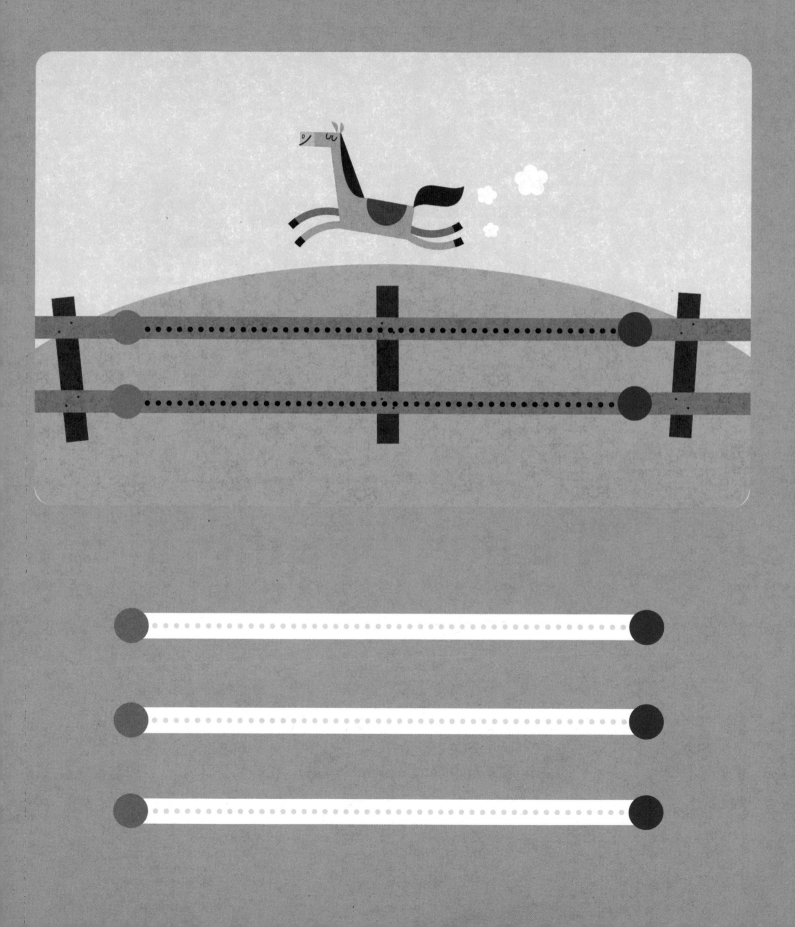

The sun shines down onto the crops.
Draw diagonal lines from dot (●) to dot (●).

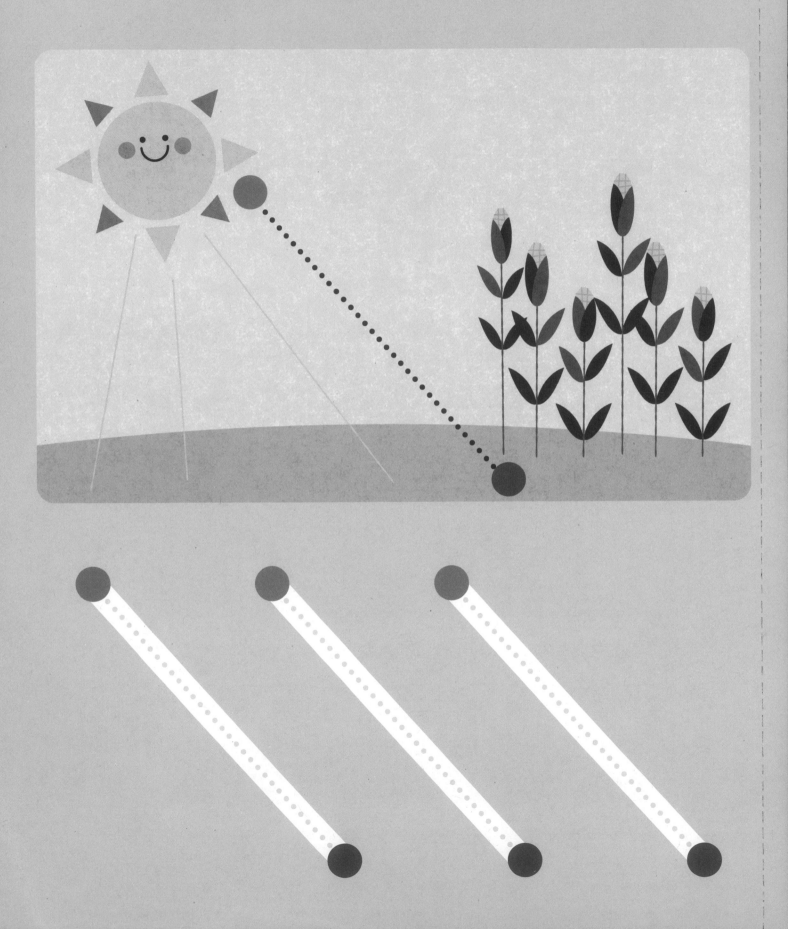

Farm workers rake the soil.
Draw diagonal lines from dot (●) to dot (●).

Sheep's wool looks like fluffy clouds.
Draw curved lines from dot (●) to dot (●).

Pumpkins grow on vines on the ground.
Draw curved lines from dot (⬤) to dot (⬤).

Horses eat from piles of hay.
Draw curved lines from dot (●) to dot (●).

Many farms raise cows.
Draw curved lines from dot (●) to dot (●).

A curvy dirt road leads to Farmer Bill's barn. Draw curvy lines from dot (●) to dot (●).

Tractors have big round tires.
Draw circle lines from dot (●) to dot (●).

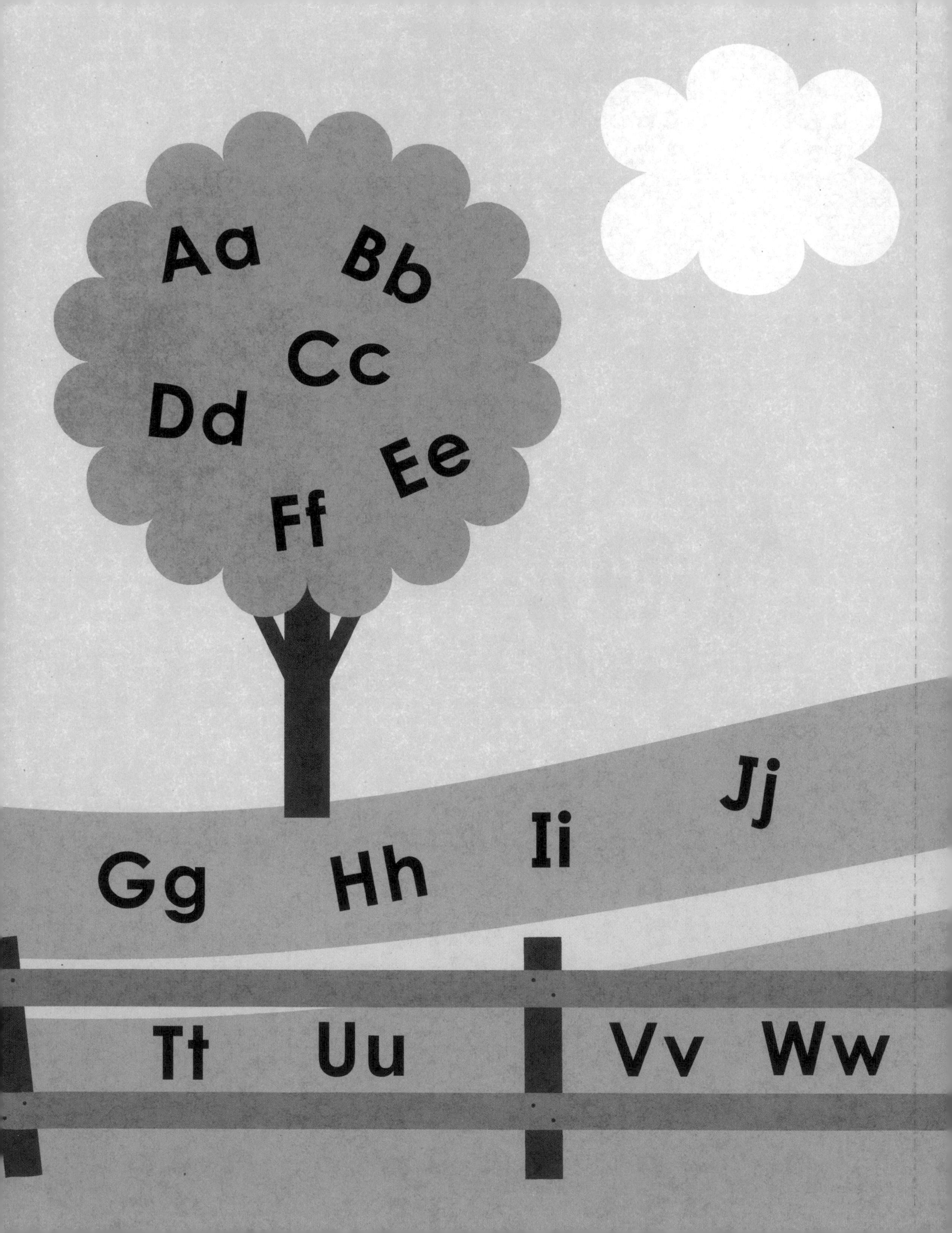

Aa Bb

Cc

Dd

Ee

Ff

Gg Hh Ii Jj

Tt Uu Vv Ww

The letters of the alphabet are all over Farmer Bill's farm!

Kk Ll Mm Nn Oo

Pp Qq Rr Ss

Xx Yy Zz

Annie eats an apple.
Trace the As.

Aa

Practice writing uppercase A.

Practice writing lowercase a.

Farmer Bill wears brown boots in the barn.
Trace the Bs.

Practice writing uppercase B.

Practice writing lowercase b.

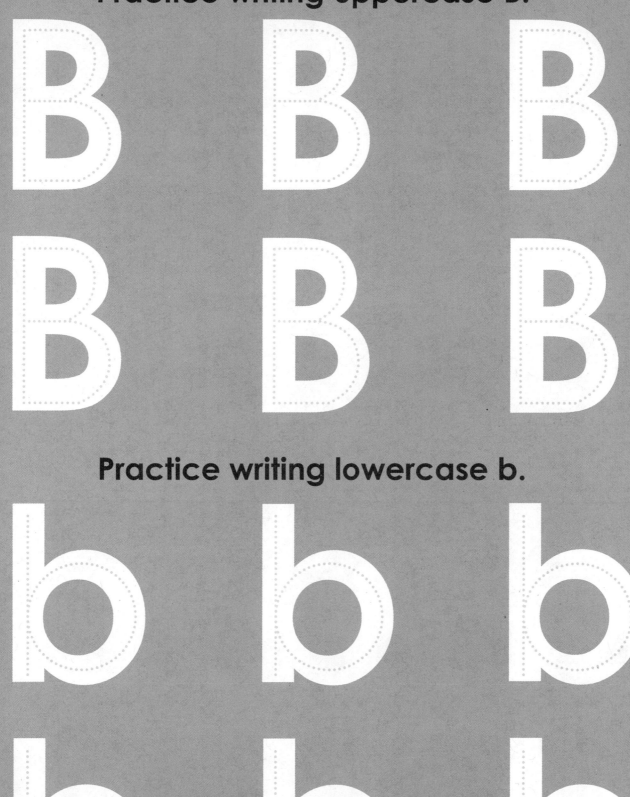

Farmer Bill's combine collects corn crops.
Trace the Cs.

C c

Practice writing uppercase C.

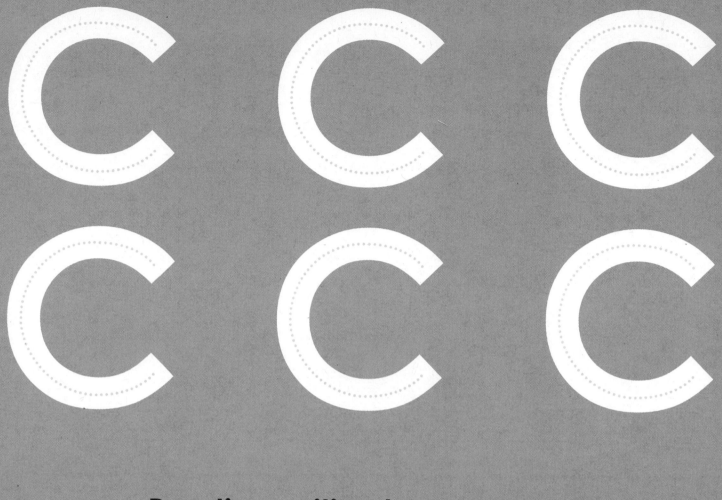

Practice writing lowercase c.

Farmer Bill's dog likes to dig in the dirt. Trace the Ds.

Practice writing uppercase D.

Practice writing lowercase d.

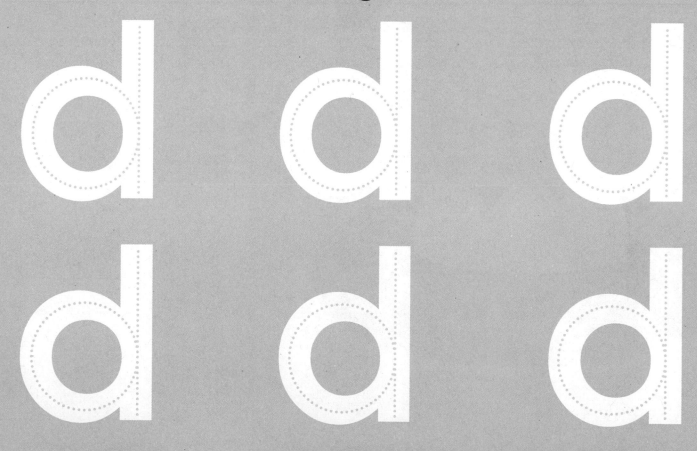

Farmer Bill gathers eggs from each hen.
Trace the Es.

Practice writing uppercase E.

Practice writing lowercase e.

Farmer Bill fixes the fence.
Trace the Fs.

Practice writing uppercase F.

Practice writing lowercase f.

The goat grazes in the green grass.
Trace the Gs.

Practice writing uppercase G.

Practice writing lowercase g.

Horses munch on hay.
Trace the Hs.

Hh

Practice writing uppercase H.

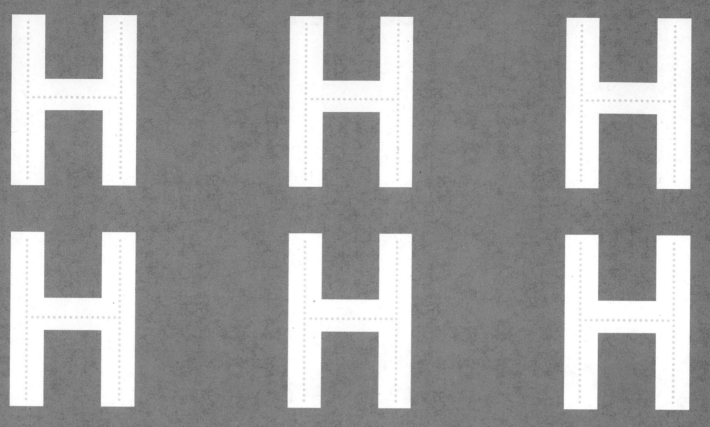

Practice writing lowercase h.

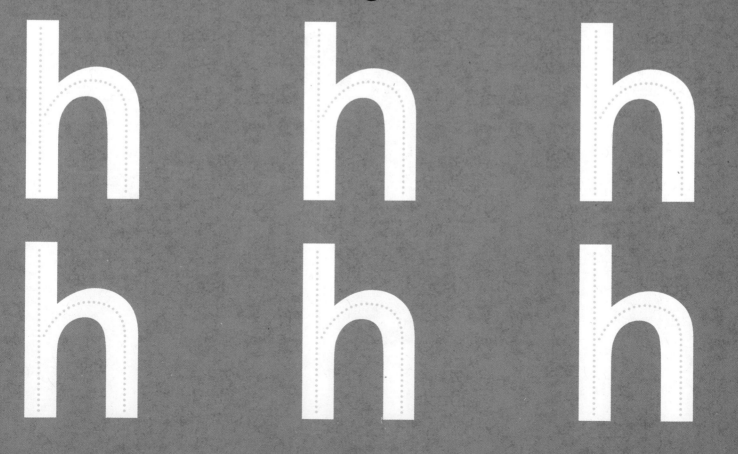

Farmer Bill eats ice cream inside his kitchen.
Trace the Is.

Practice writing uppercase I.

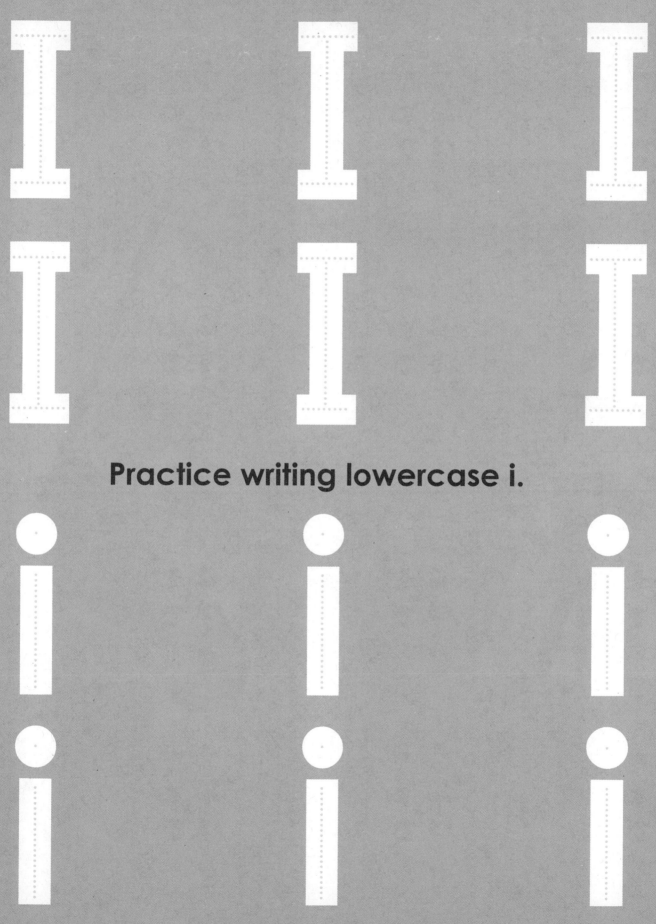

Practice writing lowercase i.

Juicy grapes make jars of jam.
Trace the Js.

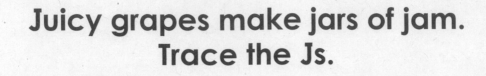

Practice writing uppercase J.

J   J   J

J   J   J

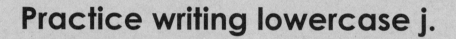

Practice writing lowercase j.

j   j   j

j   j   j

The farm has all kinds of kittens.
Trace the Ks.

Practice writing uppercase K.

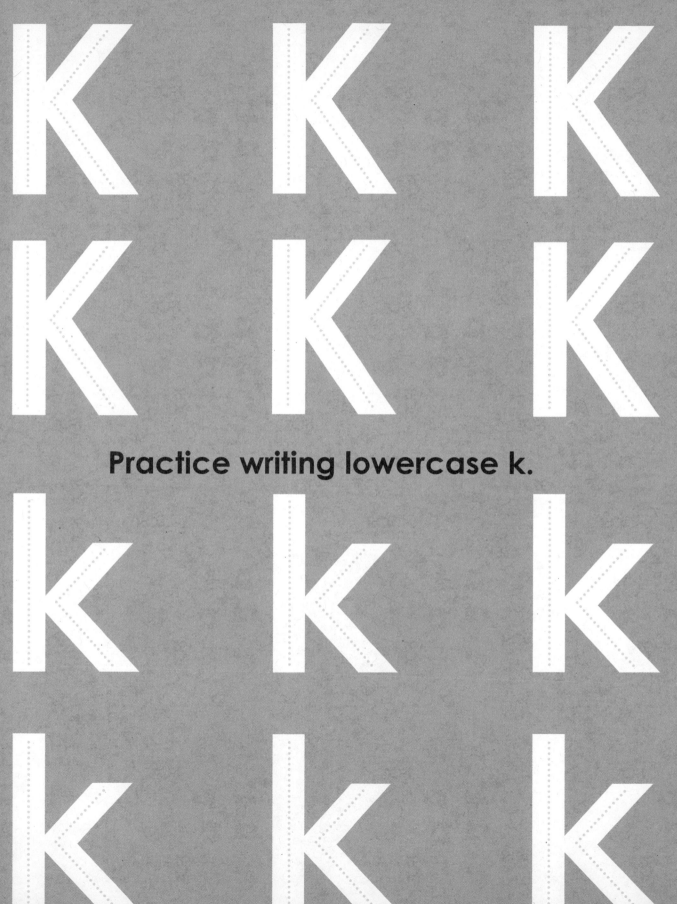

Practice writing lowercase k.

A little lamb leaps in the leaves.
Trace the Ls.

Practice writing uppercase L.

Practice writing lowercase l.

Farmer Bill sells milk at the market. Trace the Ms.

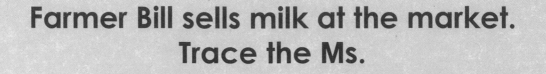

Practice writing uppercase M.

Practice writing lowercase m.

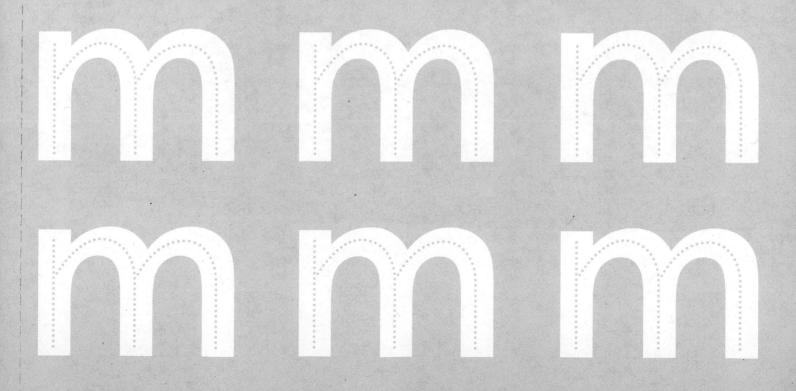

The new bird naps in a nest.
Trace the Ns.

Nn

Practice writing uppercase N.

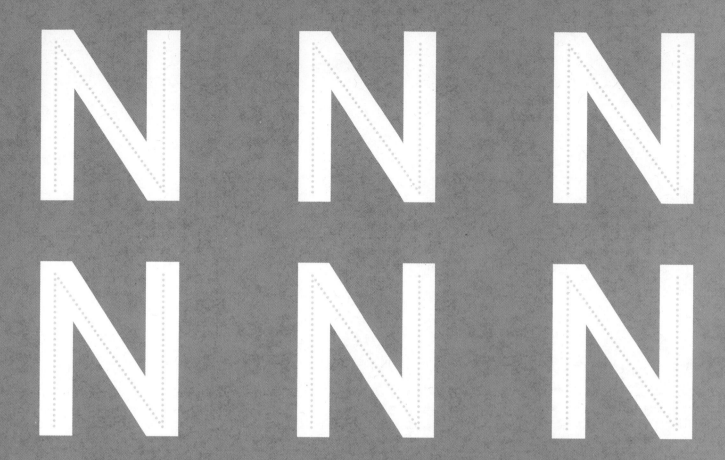

Practice writing lowercase n.

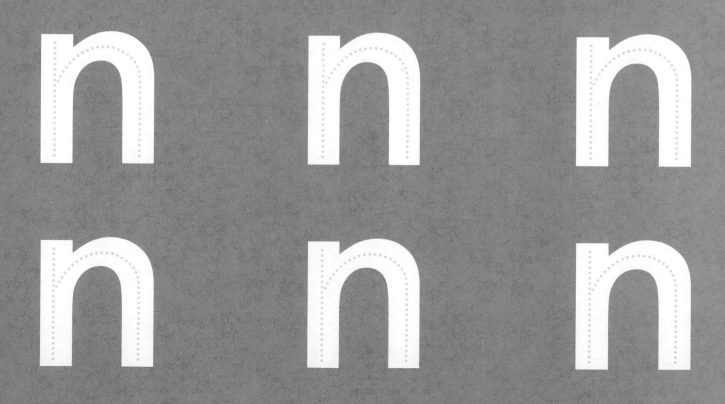

Farmer Bill wears overalls in the orange orchard.
Trace the Os.

Practice writing uppercase O.

Practice writing lowercase o.

A pink pig rolls in a puddle of mud.
Trace the Ps.

Practice writing uppercase P.

Practice writing lowercase p.

Farmer Bill quiets the quacking ducks. Trace the Qs.

Practice writing uppercase Q.

Practice writing lowercase q.

The rooster crows on the barn roof.
Trace the Rs.

Practice writing uppercase R.

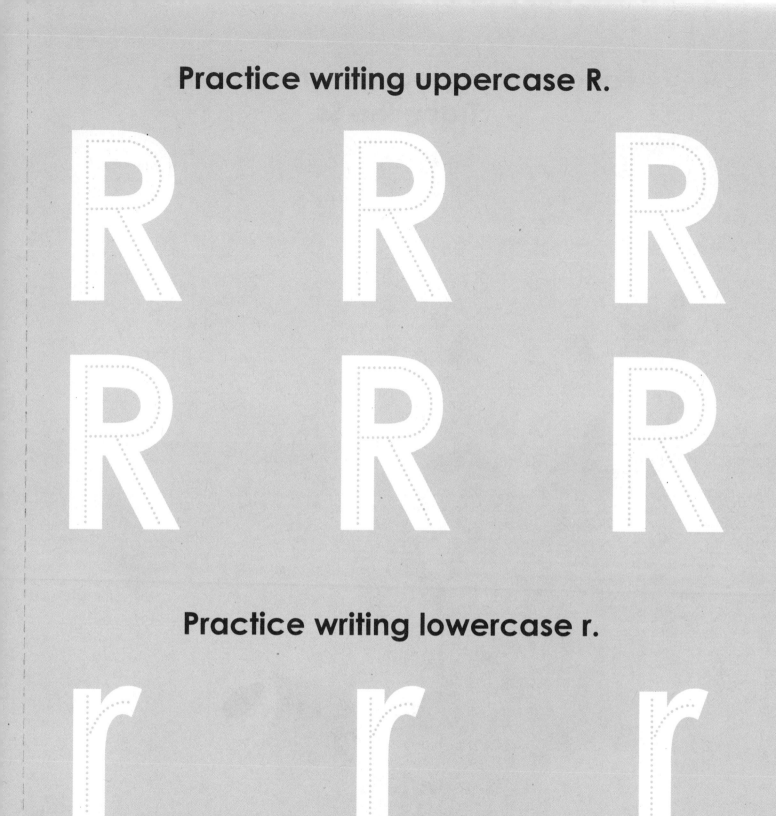

Practice writing lowercase r.

Farmer Bill sweeps the sheep stalls.
Trace the Ss.

Practice writing uppercase S.

S S S

S S S

Practice writing lowercase s.

s s

s  s

Tough tractors till the fields.
Trace the Ts.

Practice writing uppercase T.

Practice writing lowercase t.

A squirrel runs under a branch and up the tree.
Trace the Us.

Practice writing uppercase U.

Practice writing lowercase u.

Farmer Bill's vegetables are very tasty.
Trace the Vs.

V v

Practice writing uppercase V.

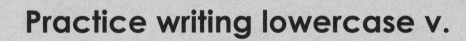

Practice writing lowercase v.

Practice writing uppercase W.

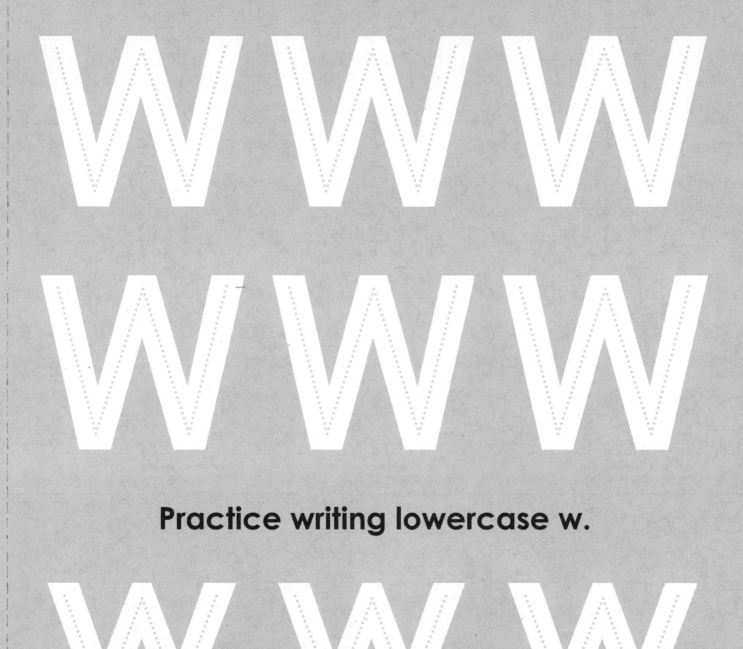

Practice writing lowercase w.

The excited fox piles fruit next to a box.
Trace the Xs

Practice writing uppercase X.

X X X

X X X

Practice writing lowercase x.

x x x

x x x

Farmer Bill makes yellow yarn.
Trace the Ys.

Yy

Practice writing uppercase Y.

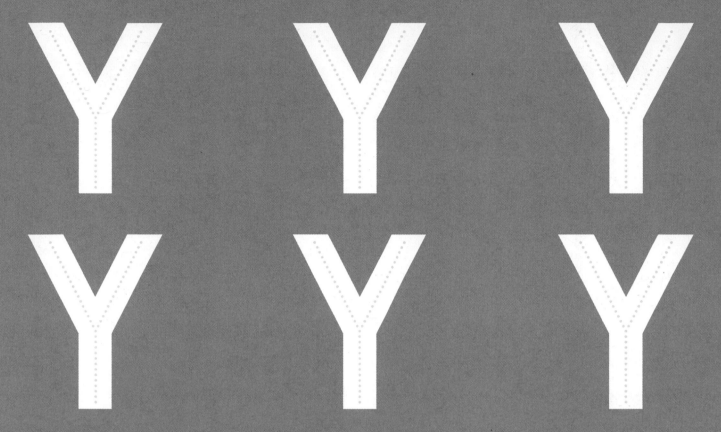

Practice writing lowercase y.

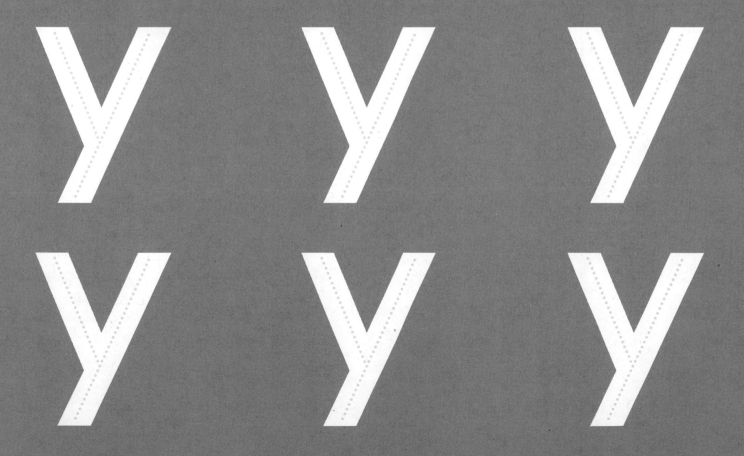

The buzzing bee zigzags by the zucchini plants. Trace the Zs.

Practice writing uppercase Z.

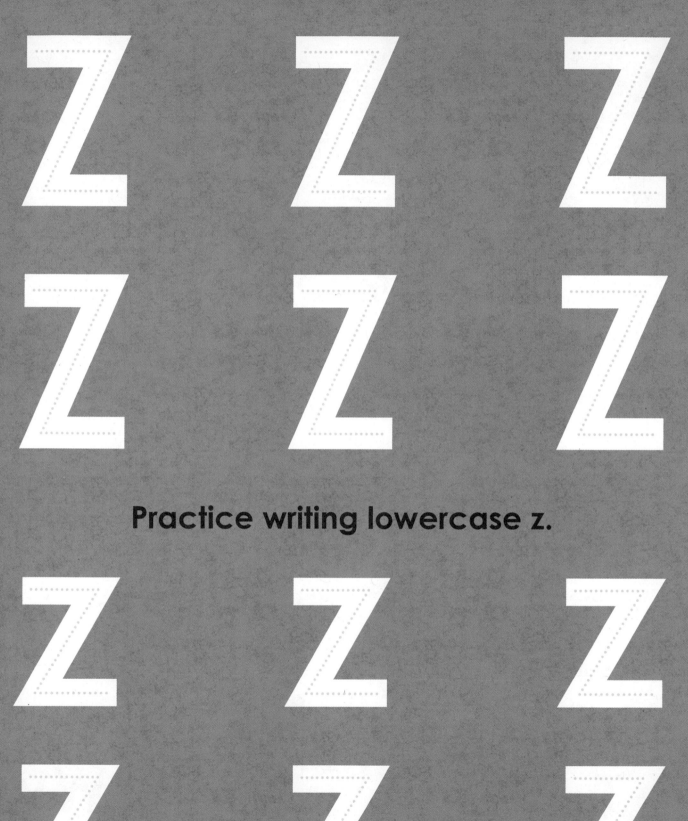

Practice writing lowercase z.

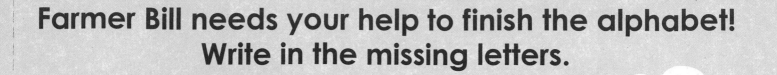

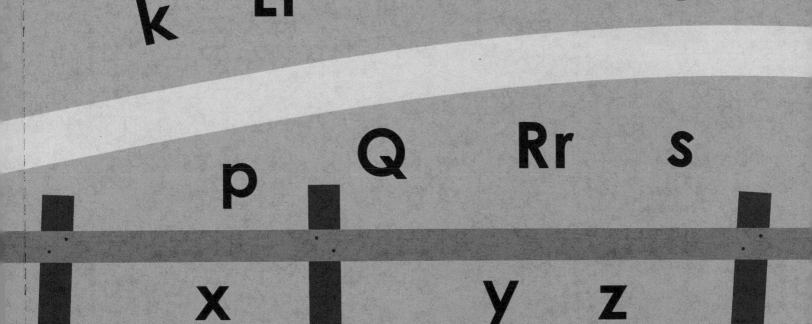

k Ll m N O

P Q Rr S

x y z

There are three farm words in the picture.
Trace each word below.
Then write each word on the blank lines.

pig

pen

mud

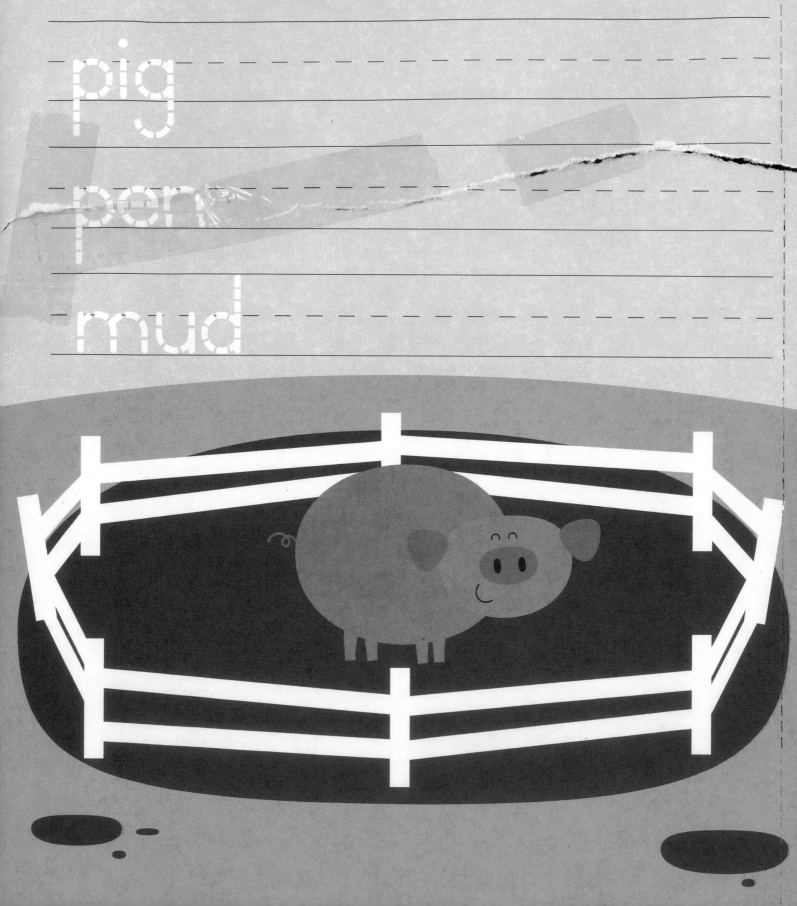

There are three farm words in the picture.
Trace each word below.
Then write each word on the blank lines.

sun

ducks

pond

There are three farm words in the picture.
Trace each word below.
Then write each word on the blank lines.

corn

field

tractor

There are three farm words in the picture.
Trace each word below.
Then write each word on the blank lines.

farmer

hat

boots

There are three farm words in the picture.
Trace each word below.
Then write each word on the blank lines.

fence

goats

barn

There are three farm words in the picture.
Trace each word below.
Then write each word on the blank lines.

dog

hole

bone

There are three farm words in the picture.
Trace each word below.
Then write each word on the blank lines.

hen

egg

nest

There are three farm words in the picture.
Trace each word below.
Then write each word on the blank lines.

pony

cat

hay

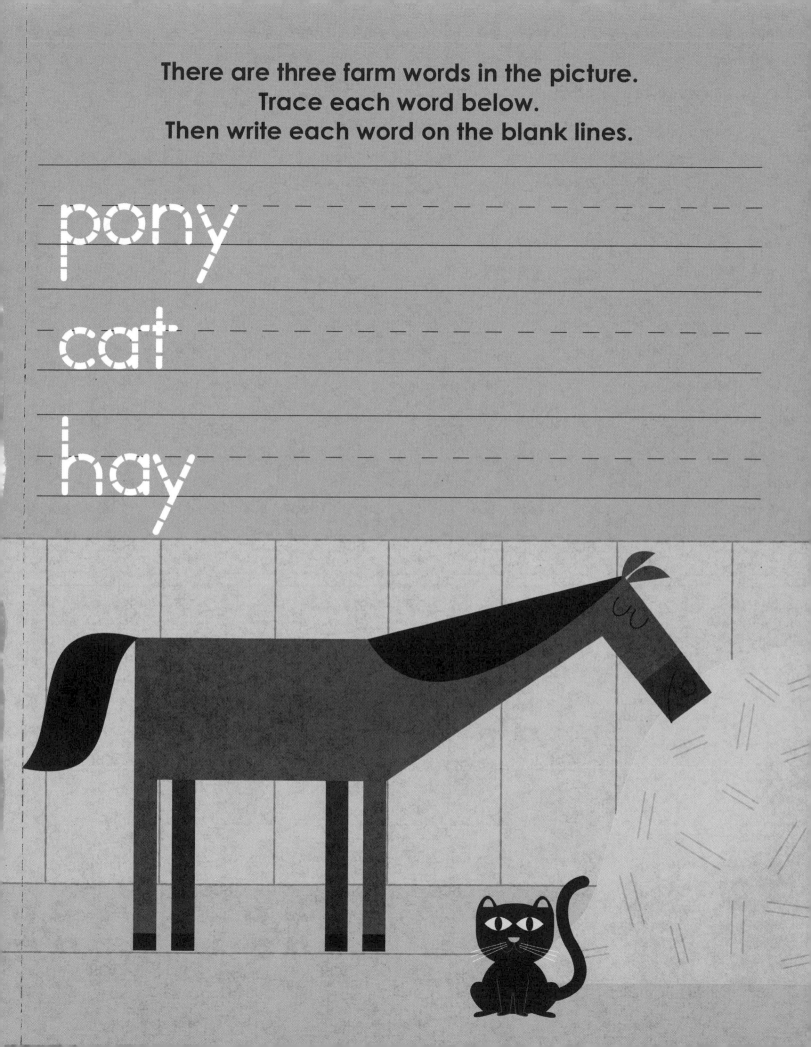

There are three farm words in the picture.
Trace each word below.
Then write each word on the blank lines.

cow

pail

milk

Congratulations!

_____

has successfully completed
Letters.